THE GIFT of ATTITUDE

10 WAYS to Change the Way You Feel

SAM GLENN

simple truths
small books. BIG IMPACT.

To my wife, who demonstrates every day the

simple and true meaning of the gift of attitude.

People will forget
what you said, people will
forget what you did, but
people will never forget
how you made them feel.

–CARL W. BUEHNER

Contents

THE
GIFT OF
Attitude
IS...

A commercial jetliner operated by Frontier Airlines was extremely delayed because of a reroute to another airport due to bad weather conditions. The pilot, crew, and passengers were on the airport tarmac, waiting there for several hours for storms to clear up so they could take off toward their final destination. The pilot recognized that the passengers were getting tense and feeling frustrated from sitting for so long. I've been in that situation and, personally speaking, watching paint dry is more thrilling.

It was almost 10:00 p.m. when the pilot, Gerhard Brandner, made a big-time choice. He decided to let everyone on the plane know that he was thinking of them and that he had their best interests at heart. He was about to create an exceptional experience

that nobody would soon forget. But I don't think he was doing it for the recognition or publicity. He was just doing what he felt was the right thing to do in the moment and doing what he would want someone to do for him. He ordered Domino's Pizza for everyone on board (136 passengers) and paid for it out of his own pocket. It was his way of sharing a little attitude, *helping others make the best of an unexpected setback.*

A caring attitude can turn things around.

This story made national headlines because it was so out of the ordinary that it had to be shared. We have all been in those moments that have us shaking our heads in frustration, but what an awesome example of how a caring attitude can turn things around—that and some cheesy pizza! Let me ask you this: Did the pilot have to order pizza for everyone? No, he did not. Did he make his airline look like the best airline in the world that day? Yes, even in the midst of frustrating setbacks. Did his actions improve the attitudes of the passengers? Oh yeah they did. He made everyone feel like they had not been forgotten and were not just another number doing business with a large company. So what was that one thing that made such a big difference? You are about to find out exactly what it is and a whole lot more in the following pages. I am excited to share with you some of the very best ways to create the most exceptional experiences for others, all with the magical touch of your attitude.

The gift of a stimulating attitude is simple yet so unique that it can make a positive difference. It makes a difference when we choose the right attitude that works for us, and it makes a

difference for others when we choose an attitude that comes from the heart. The gift of attitude is simply choosing an attitude that makes a positive impact on your life and on the lives of other people. This book is about developing your attitude sense. It's about recognizing, utilizing, and building more strength into your attitude. It's about being aware of and working on the weak points in your attitude. And finally, it's about being open to implementing new ideas about how to use your attitude to create experiences that make others feel important, valued, and cared for. Your attitude is a storymaker, and I am excited to share some of my own personal stories that highlight the gift of attitude with you. Attitude is what people know you for and will ultimately remember you for. It will be your legacy.

JUST ACKNOWLEDGING
SOMEONE WITH A SMILE
OR SIMPLE GREETING
is a gift of an
encouraging
attitude.

A friend sent me the following story, and after I read it, I thought it summed up the simplicity of how we can use our attitude as a special gift.

During my second month of nursing school, our professor gave us a pop quiz. I had breezed through the questions until I read the last one: "What is the first name of the woman who cleans the school?"

Surely, this was some kind of joke. I had seen the cleaning woman several times. She was tall, dark haired, and in her fifties, but how would I know her name? I handed in my paper, leaving the last question blank.

Just before class ended, one student asked if the last question would count toward our quiz grade.

"Absolutely," said the professor. "In your careers, you will meet many people. All are significant. They deserve your attention and care, even if all you do is smile and say hello."

I will never forget that lesson.

I also learned that her name was Dorothy.

Just acknowledging someone with a smile or simple greeting is the gift of an encouraging attitude. I love that story because it highlights that the simplest things can make others feel important and recognized. We all have the ability to do this.

THE GIFT OF CONTAGIOUS
Positivity

> # To improve a company fast, develop people fast.
>
> **—ANDRALL E. PEARSON**

*H*ere is another case of not remembering a person's name, but I will never forget her attitude and what a gift it was to me. Years ago, I met a local business owner whom I only knew as the "Vitamin Store Lady." She had told me her name (perhaps a few times), but I forgot it. I will admit that I am one of those people who struggle with remembering people's names, though I have tried to get better at it. The Vitamin Store Lady, on the other hand, was skillful at remembering me every time I walked into her shop: "Well, hello there, Mr. Sam Glenn! You look an inch taller!"

Once a month, I would stop by her vitamin and nutrition store to grab a box of protein bars, extra-strength fiber, and a bottle of Flintstones Chewable Vitamins.

When I first met the Vitamin Store Lady and encountered her positivity, I wasn't sure if it was real or whether she just had eaten way too many happy vitamins. But with each visit to her store, I discovered she was the real deal. She walked the talk, and her attitude led the way. I got to know her a little better with each visit. She reminded me of a loving grandma who enjoyed looking out for her grandkids. I think her best marketing strategy was her attitude. I was so impressed with her service, kindness, and personality that I told everyone I knew to go there. She didn't ask me to spread the word, and I didn't receive anything in return for referring people to go there. I was simply a happy customer, and happy customers like to spread the good word. The reason I told everyone was because when you have an experience that makes your day, you want others to have a similar experience, especially people you care about. I knew that anyone I told would be treated right and, as an added bonus, would leave the vitamin store feeling good about themselves and life.

When I left the Vitamin Lady's store, I always had a little more pep in my step, like my attitude had gotten a surge of positive energy. She just had that way of being so encouraging, making you smile, and making you feel good about life.

Considering what I do, speaking to organizations about the

gift of an optimistic and confident attitude as it relates to achiev-

ing success in life and at work, I began to pay closer attention to

the Vitamin Store Lady. I wanted to make sure her attitude wasn't

just for show. I wanted to find out her motivation

for treating people so well. She stood out

She stood out from the crowd with her gift of creating positive experiences for others.

from the crowd with her gift of creating

positive experiences for others. If I had

to rate her attitude, I would have put it

in the Rock Star Attitude Hall of Fame! I

might speak about and write on the subject

of attitude for a living, but the learning never ends.

This was a classroom opportunity for me, and I was going to

seize it.

On one of my routine visits to her shop, I thought it would be nice to give her a few copies of my latest book, *A Kick in the Attitude*. She was so thrilled, you would have thought that her name had just been announced on *The Price Is Right*: "COME ON DOWN! You're the next contestant on *The Price Is Right!*"

We engaged in a conversation about attitude for nearly an hour. I mostly listened. This was her time to shine, and she dazzled me with her remarkable stories. She shared about her family and all the rough times they had gone through and how they survived and became closer. She talked about why she started her business and how growing a new business can be challenging on a limited budget.

Everything she communicated somehow found a tie back to having a helpful attitude. And as if her attitude wasn't enough, she had an infectious laugh that didn't quite sound musical, but it was hilarious.

Before I left her store, she had me sign the books I gave her and reached up to give me a monster momma-bear hug. And as I was walking out the door, a friend I told about the shop was walking in. How cool is that?

As I walked to my car with the biggest smile on my face, I felt recharged. I thought, *Wow, that made my day! I feel like Tony the Tiger. I feel great, and it didn't even involve Frosted Flakes. When I give my speeches, I want others to know this feeling and experience.*

EVERYTHING
SHE COMMUNICATED
SOMEHOW FOUND
A TIE BACK TO
having a helpful
attitude.

One day during the fall, when I was traveling frequently, I had to be at the airport by 2:30 p.m. to catch a flight to Texas, so my plan was to leave the house a little early and pop into the vitamin store to get some vitamin C. By this time, whenever I went to the vitamin store, I was smiling before I even walked in the door. I knew the Vitamin Store Lady would be there to help me feel better with some vitamins and her contagious attitude.

The bell rang as I walked through the store door and, as I was trying to stomp off some of the snow on the doormat, something didn't seem the same. When I looked up from making sure the snow was off my shoes, I saw a white-haired elderly man working behind the counter. I had never seen him before. Was he new? I scanned the entire store quickly. The Vitamin Store Lady wasn't there. It must have been her day off, or maybe she'd run out for lunch. I grabbed a bottle of vitamin C and placed it on the counter to pay.

"How's your day going?" I asked with a smile to the man working the counter.

He only nodded and didn't look at me. "It's fine, I suppose."

The man seemed lost, dazed, and relatively out of it. Plus, his short responses seemed cold. I thought, *If the vitamin store lady knew this guy was so gloomy serving customers, she would not be pleased.*

So I asked him if the owner would be back anytime soon. The man's head just dropped, and it was all he could do to hold it together. Now I was confused. I asked, "Are you okay, man? Do you need something?"

He slowly lifted his head, and instantly, I could see pain in his eyes as the tears welled in them, and he summoned what looked to be part of a smile but not quite. And in a soft, gentle tone that was barely above a whisper, he asked, "Are you by chance the motivational speaker guy?"

"Uhhh...yes, I am."

"I recognize you from the picture on your book. My wife, who owns this shop, talked about you all the time. She shared your book with me also."

"Oh, so you're her husband. It is so good to finally meet you! Your wife mentioned you in a few of her stories...but all good stuff though."

He half smiled and said, "Yeah, she has some good stories, and we will sure miss her."

"Huh? What happened?"

And then he said, "My wife started to get sick a few weeks ago, and we found out she had advanced leukemia. We started treatment, but it was too late. She passed away four days ago. I am here trying to keep her store running. She always looked forward to when you would stop in. She talked about your book and how you would make her day by making her laugh."

The best form of marketing is creating a **GREAT EXPERIENCE!**

—SAM GLENN

My stomach just dropped. I got that sick feeling, and I'm sure there was a look of pure shock on my face. I stayed for as long as I could to offer some comfort and support. Before I left the shop, I told him, "Your wife was always so nice to me and had such an amazing attitude. She always made my day, and her attitude was such a gift."

The legacy of her attitude will live on.

He let out a little breath and had a look of remembrance, as if he could see his wife right in front of him. "Yes, sir, she was a gift to us all."

I feel bad that I did not remember her name, but I know one thing for sure: I will never forget her attitude. She used her attitude to grow her business. She used it to get through rough times with her family. She used it to be a great wife and to raise her kids. She used it to make a customer's day. She used it to be a friend. She used it up until the end, but the legacy of her attitude will live on. That, my friend, is an example of how you can use your attitude as a gift.

YOUR
Attitude
IS EITHER IN
THE WAY OR
MAKING A WAY

I was waiting in the service line at Meijer, our local super-market. They had multiple people helping customers who were returning items. Since they ship postal packages there, and the post office was on the other side of town, I thought I would pop in really fast and ship a few book orders.

"Next! Can I help you, sir?"

"Yes, I would like to mail out a few packages priority mail please."

"Okay... Uh... Sir, I think someone is trying to get your attention."

I looked over my shoulder and observed a woman giving me some major stink eye, that unpleasant glare someone gives you when they are not happy with you. She was glaring at me like I just stole her puppy or borrowed her car, returned it on empty, and left

crumbs all over the seat. I was immediately confused, because I wasn't aware that I had done anything to deserve the stink eye, so I inquired, "Yes, can I help you?"

With a scowl and a huff of breath, she said, "Yeah. You're in my way! Move your big butt, Bigfoot! I can't move! You need to move!"

My eyes doubled in size, as I was a bit taken aback by the words she had just thrown at me; they were like an unexpected snowball to the face. I did a quick scan of the area behind where I was standing, and it was apparent that there was at least five feet of extra room between me and the other customers waiting in line. I started to mildly laugh, because it seemed so out of the ordinary that someone would speak that way to anyone, especially since there was so much room to move past me. She could have pushed two or three full carts through the space. For a split second, I didn't know if she was joking and recognized me from my speeches. But after a few more seconds went by, it was clear she was dead serious about her request/command for me to relocate my Bigfoot-like big butt.

She was pushing a cart that was overflowing with groceries, and for some very unusual and outrageous reason, she didn't think there was enough room to move past me. So, to rectify the situation, I gracefully apologized to her and made my best attempt to squeeze closer toward the service counter, so she would have enough room to move past me.

However, the vibe I got from this lady told me that she was in an awfully bad mood, feeling miserable, and had a craving to share those negative sentiments with others. I just happened to be in the path of the tornado, or her tornado-like attitude at least. That's the thing about people who are gloom and doom—they want others to be miserable too.

The woman who had just belittled me in public had an odd look to her. And trust me, you know the look. I call it the *look of choice.* Every day, we get to choose our own attitude and how we will use it in our personal lives and at work.

As the cranky lady rolled her cart past me, she wanted to leave one final impression. She huffed at me. It was the sound I imagine the real Bigfoot might make. It was an actual huff of breath to

EVERY DAY, WE GET TO CHOOSE OUR *own attitude* and how we will use it in our personal lives and at work.

let me know one last time that she was not my number one fan. Even though I had done nothing wrong, said nothing wrong, and had no intention of doing anything wrong, I just happened to be in the path of her negative attitude. I turned back to the kid helping me at the service desk, and we both had a similar look—our eyes were practically bugging out from what we just witnessed. The other customers waiting in line were shaking their heads in disapproval at what they just observed in the epic battle of positive versus negative.

Let me ask you this: Have you ever encountered someone like this cranky lady? Did it put a hiccup in your day? Did you think, *Stubbing my toe would be a joy compared to having to deal with this person*? Maybe you thought, *Why do people have to act like that?*

Why are they so negative and feel inclined and entitled to make others feel the same?

It's frustrating, I know. And if you don't address it the right way, it can eat you up and turn your attitude rotten, like bananas that have sat out too long.

EXTERMINATE
Attitude
TERMITES

*T*he cranky woman who told me I have a big butt and called me Bigfoot was gone from the scene, but her negative impact was still there, resonating with everyone. A woman who had been standing in line waiting walked up to me and quietly said, with a gentle smile, "It's OK, young man. Some people just wear their underpants too tight. That woman didn't need to act that way toward you. Don't let it eat you up. You handled it perfectly."

Moments like that make me smile. She was what I call an *Attitude Warrior.* Attitude Warriors swoop in and lift you up when someone tries to knock you down with their negativity. She was giving me a

> **When you choose the right attitude, it becomes a gift to yourself.**

piece of her encouraging attitude to counter the negative effects of the cranky lady's attitude.

I have a little philosophy that goes like this: *Your attitude is either in the way, or making a way, and you determine which every day.*

When you choose the right attitude, it becomes a gift to yourself. When you choose the right attitude and give it away, it becomes a gift to others. When you use your attitude the right way, it becomes one of your greatest assets. When we choose the right attitude, it becomes an unstoppable force that partners with our efforts to achieve our goals. The right attitude opens new doors and seeks out the best solutions when faced with setbacks. Our attitudes are always at work—working for us or against us. Our attitudes work diligently through our abilities, education, and experiences. Every day, we get to choose the face of our attitudes, to be positive or to be average and negative. Our attitudes are communicators. They communicate who we are and what we are about. The same is true for whatever organization you work for—your attitude drives your organization's image, brand, and culture. Are people lining up outside your door or turning away and going on to the next one?

Unfortunately, a positive attitude doesn't stop tough times from knocking at your door, but it does give you the mental muscle to deal with difficulties more effectively than a negative attitude. When you choose the right attitude, it becomes a gift you give to yourself; when you share the right attitude with others, it becomes a generous gift to them. Every day and in every way, we are giving our attitude away to others.

So the questions I have for you are these:

* Do others recognize your *attitude* as a gift or a nightmare?

* Is your *attitude* working for you or against you?

* Does your *attitude* make people happy that they work with you, know you, bumped into you, or do business with you?

* Which takes up more space in your *attitude*: drama and negativity or positivity and optimism?

* Do you use your *attitude* in a way that makes a difference?

True and genuine Attitude Warriors are people who place an incredible amount of emphasis, priority, and substantial worth on having a positive attitude. They know for a fact, *a fact*, that their attitudes are relevant to everything in their personal and work lives. They understand that their atti-tudes play the lead role in everything and that, if it is not working for them, then it is costing them.

Are you using your attitude as a gift?

Think about your attitude for just a moment and how it communicates to others on a daily basis—to family, coworkers, customers, strangers you may encounter at the service desk, in traffic, and to yourself. Are you using your attitude as a gift? Are you choosing an attitude that is a gift to yourself? Taking a moment to reflect on this will enhance your attitude awareness. It will give you a greater sense of how you are using your attitude.

A CLASSIC
Attitude
SHOWDOWN

I finished paying to ship out my book orders at the service desk, turned, and made my way to the exit. I knew that I shouldn't let how the cranky lady had treated me get to me. One of my biggest pet peeves is people who are rude and display the least amount of care and courtesy toward others. That unhelpful attitude is reflected in the level of work they do in the workplace. Believe me, it's quite evident. They are what you might call clock punchers. They show up to work, punch the time clock, and automatically put the mental cruise control on until they clock out. They may show up physically, but everything else is on vacation or sitting on the couch

> That unhelpful attitude is reflected in the level of work they do in the workplace.

at home eating chips. We don't always know what the internal issues are that cause people at work to display mediocre behavior, but as customers, we hear and witness disheartening stories every day in our experiences of poor service. Have you ever been treated so poorly that you wondered how the company was still in business? Have you ever thought, *Is that how you treat a paying customer, a loyal customer, a repeat customer, a customer with cash?*

Sometimes it seems that when we are treated poorly, we let it eat us up. We can't stop thinking about it, and it becomes a negative distraction. I call that *getting infected with attitude termites.* That is what attitude termites do—they get into our minds and just eat away at our positive perspectives until we start the *stinking-thinking process.* I started thinking of things I could have said back to her at the service desk or what I would say if I saw her again. I wanted to buy her fiber as a special gift. Instead of focusing on the rest of my day and the plans I had, I was stressing and replaying a past negative experience. I was letting the cranky lady win the battle for my attitude. This is why it is so important to work on feeding your attitude positive stuff every day, so it becomes immune to attitude termites. I will share some ideas on that in the following pages.

The thing about attitude, and I will say it over and over, is that our attitude is our choice. You choose your attitude in how you do your work, treat others, and respond to situations. Erin

Greenawald said it best: "Don't spend your time trying to get even with others, but rather choose to get ahead."

Oftentimes, if we dwell long enough on the negative things people do and say, it builds up the desire to give them a taste of their own treatment. That is called getting even. Attitude Warriors are about getting ahead. Life will present you with many opportunities to choose getting even or getting ahead. When I walked out the exit doors of Meijer, I was about to be presented with that opportunity.

YOU CHOOSE YOUR ATTITUDE IN HOW YOU **do your work, treat others, and respond** *to situations.*

THE WAY
OF AN
ATTITUDE
Warrior

*T*he exit doors to the store opened, and once I stepped out into the sunny, cool day, I took a deep breath and let go of what had just happened inside. I started walking toward my truck, looked at my phone to see what time it was, and then glanced up to remotely unlock my doors. But, to my surprise, I saw the cranky lady in front of me, about twenty yards away, on the ground and struggling to get up. She looked hurt. This was the woman who just informed me and half the store that I had genetic ties to Bigfoot. I had a choice: Did I get even and blurt out, "Hey you, crazy, cranky lady! That's what you get for being so mean! And if I look like Bigfoot, it's because I

My attitude is my greatest asset— my superpower for making a difference.

haven't shaved in four days!"? Or did I get ahead by demonstrating the way of an Attitude Warrior? There was a time in my life when I had very little understanding of attitude's impact and would have been reactive and said some things to get even. But now my attitude is my greatest asset—my superpower for making a difference, my most relevant tool for facing negativity, and my closest companion in the pursuit of my ambitions. My attitude is now working by choice, rather than by random chance. Nobody other than me can choose my attitude and how I will apply it to life. That is my ownership, and it can be yours.

> It was an opportunity for me to be an Attitude Warrior and plant the example of what the right attitude is all about.

She was on the ground and looked hurt. At first, I thought she may have gotten into a physical altercation with someone in the parking lot and lost. But nobody was around, and I didn't see any cars screeching their tires to hightail it out of there. There, lying on the ground, holding her leg in pain, was the cranky lady who had just embarrassed me, talked down to me, was rude and negative, and told me my butt was oversized. Some might have chalked it up to karma, but I saw it as something else. It was an opportunity for me to be an Attitude Warrior and plant the example of what the right attitude is all about. She tried to give me some of her attitude, and it didn't work. I sent her attitude termites scrambling. This was an open door for me to give her the gift of my attitude.

I rushed over to her and asked, "Are you okay?"

Painfully, she responded, "I lost my balance and fell on my knee."

"Okay, are you able to stand up at all?"

"I think so."

"Grab my arm with both hands, and I'll lift you up."

And, just like that, I lifted her up off the ground. I felt more like Superman in the moment. She bent over to rub her knee and brush off the dirt. I remember thinking it was a good thing she was wearing jeans or her knee would have been shredded from the concrete parking lot. She slowly limped next to me as I pushed her cart to her car and assisted in loading everything into the trunk. I asked again if she was okay, and she nodded with a painful expression,

THAT BOOST OF POSITIVITY WILL ASSIST US IN THINKING POSITIVELY **and making choices that** *reward us.*

grabbed my hand, and patted it a few times in a gesture of appreciation and softly said, "Thank you, sir."

She gave me the one-motion wave as she slowly drove out of the store parking lot, and I nodded back at her with a half smile—almost like a superhero would do in the movies. It felt good to do the right thing. Even though she didn't apologize for calling me unnecessary names in the store, I was content with the outcome. I would like to think that maybe I did something for her that restored a little hope in humanity and made her think that not all people are bad. I don't know her story, but who knows? Maybe the attitude termites ate up all her positive perspective, and she just became comfortable with being cranky, and that was how she lived every day. It was evident that her attitude was not working for her. And so I stepped up, and I gave her some of mine. That is what it means to give others the gift of your attitude. I am an Attitude Warrior, and so my attitude is my greatest strength and superpower. I choose to use it in ways that help everyone win.

Sometimes, to impact our world, our cultures, our workplaces, and our lives, we just need a little infusion of positivity to clear away some of the negative fog that prevents us from thinking clearly. That boost of positivity will assist us in thinking positively and making choices that reward us, instead of leading us to the garbage dump of regret. A little positivity can permeate our interactions with others and be one of the most incredible gifts someone can receive. When you give someone the gift of

> **A little positivity can permeate our interactions with others and be one of the most incredible gifts someone can receive.**

a promising attitude, it infuses their life with renewed energy and becomes a memorable story to remember and live by. Attitude Warriors understand that sometimes our attitudes can be drained of strength and that we need to take the time to recharge. We cannot live at our best and reach new peaks when operating on empty, so you have to ask yourself this: *What is the consequence of not taking the time to recharge my attitude? What is the consequence of not taking the time at work to recharge?* Once you answer those questions honestly, you will begin to see greater value in your attitude. You will begin to hold it up to the light like a fine diamond. Instead of letting it run on zero and begin collecting dust, you will start to make it a bigger priority.

An Attitude Warrior also recognizes that when someone's attitude isn't working for them or others in a favorable way, sharing a little bit of their own positive attitude can make all the difference in the world.

·····❧·····

That is the gift of attitude!

·····❧·····

WHAT WAS ONCE WORTH PENNIES IS NOW

Priceless

I can relate to the cranky lady, and the reason I can relate so well is I used to have an attitude similar to hers. My attitude was in the way and working against me and what I wanted in life. I didn't place a high value on my attitude. *Attitude* was a word that was so overused and misused that it didn't seem relevant to me. There was a time when, if you'd asked me to appraise my attitude, I would have said it was worth pennies. But I am no longer the same person. I don't think the same way now.

As the song "Amazing Grace" states, "I once was blind, but now I see."

If you have read any of my other books or know my story, you will know that I wasn't always the most positive person in the world. I didn't buy into this attitude stuff.

Consequently, I became an expert on negativity and learned quickly that a negative attitude doesn't get you hired, promoted, or attract the right people into your life. I was sleeping on my mom's living room floor, working nights as a janitor, and letting the attitude termites eat up any ambition or dreams I might have had for myself. I was depressed, defeated, and filled with doubt. I had taken ownership of my grandfather's business and, due to some unfortunate circumstances, lost it all. I was broke, in debt, and homeless. My mom was generous enough to let me stay with her in her apartment until I was able to get back on my feet. My bed was the living room floor for over two years.

A good friend took me out for some coffee, which I could not even afford, and we began to talk about how my attitude had become the root of most of my problems. With his encouragement, I started to make a concentrated effort to fix it. As I did, my life changed. How I handled adversity changed. How I treated others changed. I wasn't always trying to think negatively. As I explored this attitude stuff a little more wholeheartedly, I learned that it really is a big deal. It saddens me when people miss how relevant attitude is to the work they do and the lives they live. When giving speeches, I like to tell my audiences that I didn't choose the subject of attitude. It chose me. I was already an expert on being negative, and what I learned being in that place was valuable to my journey ahead.

> My attitude was dependent on the roll of the dice and took on the form of whatever my circumstances were.

For years, the whole concept of attitude and the role mine played in my life and work wasn't front and center in my mind. I didn't think much about it. I operated on the little information I had about attitude. Growing up, all we hear are talks, speeches, and lectures that tie back into our attitudes and how we need to change them or have the right attitude. But, for myself, I never really understood it. I just went with the flow. My attitude was dependent on the roll of the dice and took on the form of whatever my circumstances were. So when things were bad, my attitude would get bad. When things were good, my attitude was fine. It became whatever was going on. I didn't use it to overcome setbacks, make a difference, or achieve my ambitions. I just went with the flow.

Our attitudes **are more relevant** THAN YOU COULD EVER IMAGINE.

However, I do remember a small breakthrough that helped me gain a greater appreciation of attitude. It was when the doctor told my mom that she had breast cancer and that the success of her treatment would be 10 percent what the doctors did and 90 percent would be her attitude.

If that doesn't put things into perspective, I don't know what does. Our attitudes are more relevant than you could ever imagine. The moment you become aware of this and make your attitude a priority, life will never be the same. I am living proof.

I never set out to be an author or motivational speaker. I was too scared to give speeches in school, so I took zeros and Fs with enthusiasm. I was afraid of embarrassing myself and got so nervous that my heart would feel like it was going to explode. My hands would get so wet with sweat, and my neck would get so tight that it took weeks to get all the knots out.

I didn't like public speaking, so I stopped participating in anything that required it. That all changed when I volunteered to teach Sunday school to high school students. And Joe Sabah was right: "You don't have to be great to start, but you have to start to be great." I was scared, but I had a new attitude, and confidence was part of its structure, so I faced my fears and started. I never knew or could have imagined that breaking through my biggest fear would eventually lead to my calling. Beyond our fears is a world of greatness. To get there, we have to be equipped with the right attitude. If you go at your ambitions with the wrong

attitude, you will sink the moment pressure and setbacks make their appearance—and they do show up.

For the past sixteen years, I have become known as "The Attitude Guy" and have won multiple awards including Speaker of the Year and Most Outstanding Motivational Video. I credit my success to my attitude partnered with my efforts. The right attitude will either give your efforts strength or weakness. Your attitude is what feeds your efforts.

I learn more about attitude every day, and it would seem that life is never short of opportunities to put our attitude to the test. But now, instead of seeing attitude as something everyone casually bats around, it has become the cornerstone of my life and work. Attitude is a fascinating subject and more so to me because the moment I let up even a little bit and stop working on my attitude, I become susceptible to the consequences of being attacked by attitude termites—fear, doubt, laziness, excuses, anger, misery, and negativity.

I absolutely have to work on my attitude every day and make it a priority, because if I don't, I know my relationships will begin to sink; I know my business will dry up; I know I will be burned by the weight of regret. It all starts with attitude. So jumping back a little to when I said I can relate to the cranky lady at the service desk, I get why she was the way she was. I have shaken the hand of negativity enough times to know how it takes over and controls a person's personality and affects how they treat others.

THE
GIFT OF
Courtesy

No one can choose your attitude but you! Others may try, but don't let others drive your bus...off a cliff! You own your attitude!

ourtesy is the special gift of doing something for someone that they would not expect. The other day, my family was trying out a new barbecue restaurant. The owner working behind the counter scooped up a big bowl of baked beans, handed it to me, and said, "No charge. Hope you enjoy."

Courtesy is a special gift.

The owner didn't have to give me the beans. Not

only did he give me the beans, but he also gave me the gift of courtesy. Courtesy may be holding a door open, letting someone merge in traffic, or just helping someone in any way.

Once, after boarding an airplane and sitting down, my legs were pressed into the seat in front of me, and I was miserable and cramped. It seemed to be a full flight, so I knew I had no chance of moving and finding a better seat. I just accepted that I would have to deal with it for a few hours. When everyone had boarded and they went through the safety briefing, a flight attendant walked up to me, smiled, and said, "Hey, Mr. Long Legs, you want to move? I have a seat up here that may work better for you."

I wasn't expecting someone to do that for me at

all. That had never happened to me in my sixteen years of traveling, so for someone to be aware and notice that I was cramped and to go out of their way to find me a new seat was such a gift.

I asked my wife which act of courtesy stands out in her mind as her favorite. She said, "Well, it would be nice if people would hold the door as you are going in or out of a building. When you have a big diaper bag and are carrying a baby and car seat, it is always nice when someone waits just a few seconds longer and holds the door. Sadly, most people don't do that; they just let the door slam into me."

> Do you want your attitude and behaviors coming back to you and multiplying?

I was thinking it would be cool if we instituted a courtesy law. If people go out of their way to be rude to you, then they owe you twenty dollars. And for every act of courtesy, twenty dollars magically appears in your pocket. Could you imagine if that were the case? Imagine the shift in how people would treat each other and how much more often people would go out of their way to be courteous to others. Actually, I kind of think there is a system like this already set up—it's called *karma.* Karma is the belief that whatever you send out to others in your attitude and behaviors will come back to you multiplied. Think about that. Do you want your attitude and behaviors coming back to you and multiplying? It makes you think a little and gives you a little more awareness.

EVERY NOW AND THEN, SOMEONE STEPS UP AND DOES SOMETHING SO OUT OF THE ORDINARY **that it leaves you** *speechless.*

> **Courtesy is one of the best gifts we can give to others.**

And there are times when we don't intend to do something discourteous to others. I was driving in downtown Indianapolis and accidently cut someone off so I could pull into a McDonald's to grab a coffee. I pulled up to the drive-through and I could see in my mirror the person I had cut off. He didn't seem too happy. So, when I pulled up to the window to pay for my coffee, I gave the drive-through cashier an extra twenty dollars and said, "I accidently cut off the guy behind me and want to pay for his meal. If there is any change left over, you can put it in the donation jar for the Ronald McDonald House."

The lady took the money and jokingly said, "Wow, I need to have someone like you cut me off! That is really nice of you."

I was trying to fix what I did wrong by doing something right. It wasn't much, but when I pulled out of the parking lot, I looked back to see how the person I had cut off responded. First, it was a look of confusion; then, the cashier pointed at me, and when the gentleman in his car looked over, he waved and had the biggest smile ever.

The gift of courtesy is often a surprise to many. Every now and then, someone steps up and does something so out of the ordinary that it leaves you speechless. I saw an article about people who took courtesy to a whole new level. One person put a bunch of change in an envelope and taped it to a vending machine with a note that said, "Get whatever you want on me!" Another person

noticed some litter in a parking lot and walked around, picked it up, and disposed of it. I could list story after story. Courtesy is one of the best gifts we can give to others. It may not be much in our mind, but to someone else, it can be everything.

One last story on this subject. I want to share what happened after my wife and I had our first baby. The weather was getting nice, and my wife started to take our daughter for a walk in the stroller around the pond by our home. Next to the pond, there was some major construction going on, and you could hear hammering, pounding, drilling, and trucks working all day long. However, the construction crew noticed my wife walking by with a baby, and everyone stopped working, shut down the machines, and didn't make any noise or start back up again until she had passed. Wow, that was cool! We never expected them to halt production for a few minutes so as not to upset a baby. That was just awesome. That is the gift of courtesy! It is an unexpected surprise and means everything.

THE GIFT OF RECHARGING YOUR *Attitude* BATTERIES

*W*hat drains our attitude of energy the most? Stress! Stress is caused by a number of things: changes at work, relationship issues, kids, moving, bills, money, an annoying coworker who likes to eat garlic for breakfast, family, and the list can go on and on. Research shows that a little stress is good for you, but too much built up over time will eventually hurt you.

I am sitting at the airport as I write this and just looked up to see some guy frantically scrambling to find a plug to charge his cell phone. If you think about it, the phone that he is holding (or that you have) represents years of technological advancement. Millions, if not billions, of dollars were spent to develop the technology. However, if the cell phone doesn't have that little positive

charge, it doesn't matter how much the technology cost, it will not do what it was designed to do. It's no good.

The same is true for us. I've said it before: our attitude is much like a battery that needs to be recharged from time to time. The number-one human-attitude battery drainer is stress. When the stress builds up over time, it can lead to sickness and fatigue. Sometimes too much stress can lead to mental instability and poor decision-making. Recharging your attitude is a maintenance process that leads to better emotional management.

If you are trying to give your best and are running on empty, your results will be less than average. Would you try running a marathon the day after a marathon? No way! If you did, you would not perform at your best. You need time to recharge. That is why I am always confused when organizations that want to turn a greater profit, boost productivity, and improve performance don't take the time needed to do a little attitude maintenance. The biggest disservice to any bottom line is when the recharge process is overlooked or given a low appraisal.

The achievements of an organization are the results of the combined effort of each individual.

–VINCE LOMBARDI

When you value positive people engaged in positive action, you have to make the recharge process a significant priority. An empty, stressed, and fatigued attitude cannot win a worthwhile race. As a result, you and your organization's potential is never tapped. So the big question is: How can you recharge your attitude batteries?

Nothing great was ever achieved without enthusiasm.

–RALPH WALDO EMERSON

IF YOU CANNOT DO GREAT THINGS, **do small things** *in a great way.*

—NAPOLEON HILL

Recharging your attitude can be simple, fun, and highly rewarding. It is more effective than pounding caffeine drinks all day. Don't get me wrong. I love my coffee, but recharging our attitude is what puts authentic and substantial fuel into your mental factory, and we need that fuel to operate at our best. Let me highlight a few simple and easy ways that work to recharge our attitude batteries.

1. **Go for a walk.**

2. Take a **fifteen-minute break** to clear your mind. Stretch and take a few deep breaths.

3. Read positive **quotes**.

4. Plan for more **sleep** at night or take a twenty-minute nap. Did you know that Thomas Edison had a cot in his office, and when he felt like he needed a mental recharge, he would stop working and take a short nap?

5. Get away. Plan a time to **get away** for a weekend or a few days and decompress by doing something fun for yourself.

6. Lighten up. Choosing to have a **sense of humor** is my favorite way to recharge and release stress.

DON'T MISS THE LITTLE GIFTS THAT *Surround* YOU DAILY

> Progress is impossible
> without change, and
> those who cannot change
> their minds cannot
> change anything.
>
> —GEORGE BERNARD SHAW

I believe that, in order to give the gift of attitude, we have to develop a greater awareness for the gifts that surround us every day. This is how we develop a better sense and ability to recognize greatness in others. The gifts of life are always circling us, but sometimes we get so busy and hyperfocused on

stuff that we miss some pretty awesome things. I remember attending a fundraiser that Jim Belushi would be attending for a short while. I had wanted to meet him and get my picture taken with him for years, so I kept a keen lookout for him because I didn't want to miss my chance. The night moved on without any sign of him, so to pass the time, I sat in a chair and started to play a game on my phone, Candy Crush. After playing for nearly ten minutes, I heard people talking over my shoulder, but I didn't look up to see who they were. Who happened to be among them? Jim Belushi! He said to my friend, "Wow, he is really into that game. He hasn't looked up once." I was so bummed that I missed that amazing opportunity and that it was sitting right there over my shoulder. If you don't pay attention, you never know what you will miss.

If you don't pay *attention,* YOU NEVER KNOW WHAT YOU MIGHT MISS.

Here is another story that illustrates my point: A man sat at a metro station in Washington, DC, and started to play the violin; it was a cold January morning. He played six classical pieces for about forty-five minutes. During that time, since it was rush hour, about 1,100 people went through the station, most of them on their way to work.

As a middle-aged man walked by, he noticed there was a musician playing and slowed his pace then stopped for a few seconds to listen before hurrying on to meet his schedule. A minute later, the violinist received his first dollar tip; a woman threw the money in the till and, without stopping, continued walking by.

A few minutes later, someone leaned against the

wall to listen to him, but the man looked at his watch and started to walk again. Clearly he was late for work.

The one who paid the most attention was a three-year-old boy. His mother tugged him along, but the kid stopped to look at the violinist. Finally, the mother pulled hard, and the child continued to walk, turning his head as he walked away. This action was repeated by several other children. All the parents, without exception, forced them to move on.

In the forty-five minutes the musician played, only six people stopped and stayed for a while. Twenty-seven gave him money, but most of those continued to walk on as they did so. He collected thirty-two dollars. When he finished playing and silence took over, no one noticed. No one applauded, nor was there any recognition.

No one knew this, but the violinist was Joshua Bell, one of the most talented musicians in the world. He had begun his subway concert with one of the most intricate pieces ever written, playing a violin worth 3.5 million dollars. Three days before his playing in the subway, Joshua Bell sold out at a theater in Boston where average seats were one hundred dollars.

This is a real story. Joshua Bell playing incognito in the metro station was organized by the *Washington Post* as part of a social experiment about perception, taste, and priorities of people. They asked the following questions:

In a commonplace environment at an inappropriate hour:

1. Do we perceive beauty?

2. Do we stop to appreciate it?

③ Do we recognize the talent in an unexpected context?

One of the possible conclusions from this experience could be that if we do not have a moment to stop and listen to one of the best musicians in the world playing the best music ever written, how many other things are we missing?

THE GIFT OF
Recognition

Recognition makes people feel like rock stars. Everyone wants to know that who they are and what they do matters. One of the most empowering ways to put a positive spark in someone's attitude is to give them the gift of attitude by acknowledging them. People are so hungry for the sound of recognition and praise that they will climb buildings to fill the need. I recall reading an article about a guy who was arrested for climbing city buildings. They called him the "Human Spider-Man." People would cheer him on while he climbed, and when interviewed about what his motivation was for doing something so crazy, his response was, "I just wanted to hear the cheers."

> Everyone wants to know that who they are and what they do matters.

Recognition gives people a sense of purpose, a sense that what they are doing truly matters. Recognition is simply acknowledging the value of others and the things they do. People want to know that progress is happening because of them. They want to feel involved and a part of something worthwhile. Years ago, when I was doing a sound check for an event, a young man named Curtis had volunteered to help me set up. We worked together for about an hour, and when we were done, I told him, "Curtis, you keep doing what you do. You are a rock star! Thank you so much for your time and effort in helping me get all set up today."

He looked away to hide the tears that were building up, and I said, "Hey. You okay, man? Do I smell bad or something?"

"Yes, I'm okay. But you're the first person ever to thank and compliment me on my work around here. That just means so much to me."

Don't worry when you are not recognized,
but strive to be worthy of recognition.

—ABRAHAM LINCOLN

Another time, when I got home from a long trip, I made my way into the kitchen to grab a light snack and sit down to decompress a little. It was close to 1:00 a.m., so I was trying to be quiet. When

I opened up our pantry, I was in shock. My first thought was, *Oh boy. I'm so tired, I think I went into someone else's house.*

The pantry didn't look familiar at all. I stepped back and looked around to make sure I was in the right house. What had happened to the pantry? It looked like it had been overhauled. Someone had made it look organized, like the pantry fairy came and gave us the gift of a clean pantry and fresh, edible food.

I hadn't asked my wife to clean the pantry (because why should it be any more her job than mine?), but she had spent hours cleaning it, and it looked amazing.

So I cleaned up after my snack and crawled into bed.

"How was your event, Sam?" my wife whispered.

"It was good. Glad to be home." And then, I quietly said, "Hey, the pantry looks amazing. You did such a great job. Thank you for doing that."

She perked up, leaned over, and smiled big. "You noticed? That means so much."

"Yes, I noticed. That was amazing of you to take the time to do that. For real, thank you."

I am sure it wasn't fun for her to spend all that time cleaning the pantry when she had so many other things going on, but when I recognized her for what she did, it made it all worth it. She didn't care about how long it took or that she had to haul heavy trash bags to the garage, but what made it 100 percent worth it to her was that little recognition.

Recognition in a relationship is so vital to its growth. It is a form of love that deepens the quality and connection of the relationship. My wife practically cheers and throws a party for me whenever I change out a roll of toilet paper and put on a new roll. It doesn't seem like a big deal to me, but apparently it is to her. There are other things I do around our house that I just figure need to get done, so I do them. And my wife will write me a little note of thanks and share with me reasons why she loves me. Her recognition makes me feel special, and that is what recognition is all about. It is a gift.

> **What made it 100 percent worth it to her was that little recognition.**

Recognition works with others when you are out and about,

running errands. The other day, someone held a door open for me. I praised the person by saying, "Thank you. I love it when people are so nice and hold the door for others." He smiled and accepted the praise. And guess what he will do and be happy to do again? Hold the door for someone else. Why? Because of the praise and recognition.

THE GIFT OF
Encouragement

> Start looking for the good in others,
> and the more you look for the good in others,
> the more good you will find. Feeling appreciated
> is one of the most important needs that people
> have. When you share with someone your
> appreciation and gratitude, they will not forget
> you. Appreciation will return to you many times.
>
> **—STEVE BRUNKHORST**

After leaving the White House to resign from the highest office in the country, our late president Richard M. Nixon was so discouraged and depressed that he was actually admitted to a hospital. Filled with despair, he told his wife while in the hospital, "Patricia, I am so depressed, I wish God would let me die."

At that very moment, a nurse entered the room with a cheery smile and said, "Mr. President, have you looked out the window today?"

He was so filled with sadness because he had let his family, his country, and himself down that he had intentionally kept the curtains closed, refusing to allow any sunlight in. She said, "We really need to let some light in here, so that may cheer you up."

> **Something awesome happens when we get connected to a little encouragement.**

She went to the window, opened the curtains, and at that very moment, a plane flew across the sky with a banner. The sign simply read: *Mr. President, God loves you and we do too.*

Tears began streaming down the former commander in chief's cheeks. He said, "How long has that plane been flying today?"

"Matter of fact, it has been flying back and forth all day, waiting for your curtains to be open," the nurse said.

Something awesome happens when we get connected to a little encouragement. It makes us feel better about life and ourselves. Encouragement really gives us strength to stop thinking down and start thinking up. We gain confidence and, therefore, can tackle the biggest giants in our lives. Encouragement comes in different forms at different times.

Correction does much, but encouragement does more.

—JOHANN WOLFGANG VON GOETHE

Encouragement feeds our attitude with renewed inspiration and energy. It opens our minds to solutions when we thought there were none. Sometimes people need just a little dose of encouragement to keep moving forward.

WHOEVER IS **happy will make others** *happy too.*

—ANNE FRANK

THE GIFT OF
Negativity

I say this with the utmost level of enthusiasm—let's talk about negative stuff! Is there any real gift or good that can come from negativity? Since I used to be a very negative person, I happen to have some credible firsthand experience with this subject. Negativity is like a disgruntled employee who doesn't care, makes circumstances worse, and ends up costing the company a fortune. When you observe negativity or drama, it becomes a teachable example of what not to do and what doesn't work. We can learn from that and apply the lessons.

The consequences of negativity in life and the workplace are you lose customers; you reduce your chances for new opportunities, promotions, and bonuses; you treat others poorly; and you engage in unhealthy habits. And finally, the biggest consequence

of a negative attitude is that it's just ugly. And that isn't my opinion but rather a fact.

An ugly attitude does not have your best interests at heart. It doesn't work for you. Have you ever seen an adult throw a temper tantrum fueled with drama and thought, *How is that going to help them or make the situation better?* It won't. The wrong attitude just doesn't make happen what you want to happen. I know—I have tried and tried and tried.

> The biggest consequence of a negative attitude is that it's just ugly.

A few years ago, I was on a conference call with a company that was inquiring about having me speak at their annual conference.

One lady sternly asked, "Do you just tell people to think and be positive and everything will be good? Because our company is about more than just being positive."

Now, in situations like this, I would actually talk the group out of booking me and suggest some other speaker who would be a better fit. So in this particular case, I suggested it might be a good idea to wait until they saw me at a conference or heard more about my work in the media. That way, they could see me in action, see the audience's response, and see how happy I make my clients.

The same woman cut me off midsentence: "Mr. Glenn, we know you speak on attitude, but we are not looking for a rah-rah pep talk. We are looking for substance and content. What value or effect will your message have on our people and organization?"

So I began to explain to the five people on the conference call that my message sounds a lot more lightweight than it really is. My philosophy is that it all starts with attitude. The success and culture of an organization is driven and determined by attitude. The growth, leadership, and future of an organization all depend on attitude.

Attitude is what drives innovation, possibilities, and new ideas. Attitude is our emotional management center that determines how we handle stress and pressure and how we respond to change. Our attitude influences our level of effort and the choices we make. So I think it would be fair to say attitude is kind of a big deal.

The conference call was a little overwhelming, and I wanted to help them better understand what I do and grasp the real depth of my materials, so I decided to share an epic story that featured

THE COSTS CAN ADD UP WHEN ANY SIZE OF ORGANIZATION DOESNT' MAKE *attitude* **a top priority.**

a confrontation between a store manager and me. I wanted to highlight the costs and consequences of negative attitudes in the workplace, and this story was an excellent illustration of that. There is a bigger picture when it comes to this attitude stuff. However, it's unfortunate how the costs can add up when any size of organization doesn't make attitude a top priority. The following story is about how we can learn and gain something positive from something negative.

I walked into a major retail store with $500 cash to buy a new TV. I noticed an open-box sale and asked if I could get a reduced price to fit my budget. It was marked at about fifty dollars over my budget. They said they would have to check with the manager. They called the manager, but he didn't show up for twenty minutes. When he did arrive, he didn't greet me or ask how he could help, he just responded by saying, "What's the problem?"

Not the best comment when you don't even know if there is a problem or not. I explained my situation and most managers are authorized to give 10 percent additional discount if you ask on open-box items. So I asked. He was very rude and started shaking his head before I was even done asking. His response was, "Absolutely not, this has been discounted already." And he began to walk away.

Since I believe it is a disservice to not help this company, I created a teachable moment. Why is it okay for that manager to treat me poorly and not okay for me to speak up? Before he got

too far, I responded to him by saying, "I had $500 cash to buy a TV today. Based on how you treated me, some other company is going to get my revenue. When you treat customers poorly, that's the result. And by the way, if this was *America's Got Talent*, you would have been booed off the stage."

I had to get that last tidbit in there because he needed to know that his attitude and behavior cost his company revenue that day.

But let's do the hypothetical math. Let's say he treats a customer poorly every day—the way he treated me—for a year. Let's say that each customer is going to spend $500 each day. What did his attitude cost his company in revenue? The answer? $182,500.

Now, let's go a little farther with our math. Since that was only one store and they have 14,000 of them worldwide, what if one employee with a bad attitude treated a customer bad for one day out of the year and it cost the company one hundred dollars per customer? What did their attitudes cost their company in revenue? The answer? $1,400,000.

The cost of negative attitudes in the workplace can add up quickly.

After I shared this story about a manager named Mike, the group hired me. It crystallized the point and the value of why having positive employees engaged in positive action is so essential to growth and success. In fact, they turned out to be a fantastic organization and great people to work with, and because they trust me and I did a good job for them, they keep having me back as a guest speaker.

THE GIFT
OF MOVING
Forward

S ometimes things happen that bring a halt to everything. It's called unexpected change. Change is uncomfortable; it is inconvenient and takes time to adapt to. John C. Maxwell said, "Change is inevitable. Growth is optional." I love reading stories about people who faced the odds with courage and came out ahead. They found a way to keep moving forward when things were thrown at them and became roadblocks or setbacks. Instead of giving up and throwing in the towel, they have that "keep moving forward" attitude, and as a result, they start to see renewed possibilities for their lives and circumstances.

"Change is inevitable. Growth is optional."

I particularly love the story of a woman who ran a

successful hair salon. One day, a national chain built a salon just across the street. She could have complained, "What if they put me out of business? What will I do?" However, she decided to keep the right attitude. When the salon across the street opened, they had a big sign in the window that read, "Special: $5 Haircuts!" The woman responded with the right attitude—and it brought her more business. She put a sign in her window that read, "We fix $5 haircuts!"

I recall a time before my speaking career took off when I wasn't sure if anyone would ever call to have me speak. It had been a whole year of putting the word out there, and nobody was calling. My "keep moving forward" tank was starting to run empty. I could hear doubt and fear knocking at the door. I was just about out of money and still nobody was calling. I would pace in front of the answering machine, checking it up to ten times an hour, to see if anyone had called. I must have heard over a hundred times a day, "You have no new voice mails."

I was on the edge of giving up. I didn't have any more strength to keep moving forward.

I began to question myself. *What am I doing wrong? Maybe I'm not good enough. How am I going to make it if I fail? All I need is a chance!*

I was on the edge of giving up. I didn't have any more strength to keep moving forward. But one night, I noticed a present on the kitchen table with my name on it. It was from one of my most

treasured friends who believed in me and knew I needed some "keep moving forward" fuel. The gift was a book by Dr. Robert H. Schuller called *Tough Times Never Last, But Tough People Do!* It was autographed as well. I flipped through the pages and wedged in between several pages was $300 cash. I was floored by such a generous gift, and it wasn't so much the money or the book that inspired me, but it was the message of the gift. My friend's confidence in who I was and what I was doing inspired me to keep moving forward. It gave me hope to hold on and not to give up. I was on the edge of giving up so many times. Now, no matter what type of group I speak for, I know it would not have happened or become real had I stopped moving forward. But I couldn't have done it alone. When I was weak and out of ideas, the encouragement from loved ones inspired me to keep moving forward, to keep pressing on. Too often, there is a fight that is going on inside us. A part of us wants to throw in the towel, and the other part is saying with every last fiber, *Just a little further.*

Life is always going to throw us curveballs and changeups that throw everything off course. It is in those moments when we can start to fill up with doubts, but those are the times when we have to find the fuel to feed the fire and keep moving forward. We can learn from the stories of those in history who faced outstanding challenges—somehow and someway, they found a way. The underlying factor was they kept moving forward. Let those lessons be fuel to inspire you to keep moving forward as well.

THE GIFT OF
Integrity

*H*ave you ever been burned by someone due to their lack of truthfulness? I am going to assume yes. It hurts and weakens the bridge of trust. It ends relationships. It crushes credibility in an instant. Integrity is about communicating through your actions and attitude in such a way that people trust you. Maybe you are like me and at times have said out loud, "Who can you trust these days?" When people break the bond of honesty, it shifts your thinking to *Who can I trust?* A little truthfulness goes a long way.

We had just moved to a new state and were basically starting over from scratch. One of my priorities was to get established and set up with a new accountant. I did some Google searching,

> **A little truthfulness goes a long way.**

made calls, sent emails, and interviewed a few to see who would be a good fit for my company. After some careful consideration, I was able to narrow it down to someone I thought would have my business and family's best interests at heart. I didn't just want bookkeeping services but someone who would work well with our goals for the future. My initial conversation with the accountant I picked had me feeling secure that I had made a good choice. However, the thing about integrity is that it entails much more than our words. Our integrity reveals its true nature in our actions, choices, and behaviors. Some people try to bend the bar of integrity to justify certain actions, but integrity doesn't work that way. When you do what is right, communicate truthfully, and do what you say you will do, that is integrity in motion!

As a friendly gesture, I thought I would stop into my new accountant's office for a quick visit to introduce my wife and new baby girl. So I called him up to schedule a brief visit, and after hearing his excitement for us to stop in, my family and I got into the car and made the five-minute drive to his office. When we arrived, he welcomed us, and we chatted for only a few minutes before we were on our way.

A few days passed, and I had walked outside to grab the mail and found a letter from his office. I thought maybe they sent a letter about how great it was to meet my family, maybe something about how excited they were to work with me and an offer to answer any questions I may have had.

Those are the best letters to get from people you are about to engage in business with. I tore open the envelope and unfolded

the letter, but I didn't see any of those magic words or sentiments in it. In fact, it wasn't a letter at all—it was a bill. A bill! I scrolled to the bottom of the bill, where it stated a new balance owed in the amount of eighty dollars. I was dumbfounded because we hadn't done any work yet. So I looked at the description of the work I was being billed for, and it read: *Fifteen-minute visit with client's wife and baby.*

My mouth dropped to the ground. *Really? Are you kidding me? They sent us a bill for stopping in to say hello, and we weren't even there for fifteen minutes! Ahhh! That is some shady stuff.*

I was more than disappointed and felt like I had just gotten punched in the gut from someone I really

The gift of
integrity
IS ABOUT OWNING THE WORDS AND PROMISES YOU PUT OUT THERE.

needed to rely on and trust. Later that week, we bumped into the new accountant in the grocery store. He walked up to us with a big smile and greeted us with simple pleasant- ries. I jokingly said to him, "We would love to talk with you right now. However, we're on a fixed budget and can't afford another eighty-dollar bill to chitchat with you."

> **I had just gotten punched in the gut from someone I really needed to rely on and trust.**

He looked confused at first, and then it sunk in. His face began to turn red with embarrassment, and he got the picture. We would have been great customers for his firm for years and years, but that one simple act had cost him our business. I am not debating whether his time is valuable or not, but there is an etiquette and integrity factor involved. It made me feel that if I couldn't trust him with the little things, I definitely wouldn't be able to trust him with the bigger, more important things.

The gift of integrity is about owning the words and promises you put out there. It is communicating truthfulness. If the accountant had informed me that any office visit is an on-the-clock visit, I would have respected that guideline as his way of business. I might not agree with it, but I would have respected him and his organization a lot more had he communicated their policy.

THE GIFT OF A BETTER *You*

A friend of mine who manages a successful company shared with me his philosophy on why he buys everyone books and promotes personal improvement in the workplace.

"I want my employees to work harder on themselves than they do at their job. When they get better at who they are, they become awesome at what they do."

This reminded me of a saying that has stuck with me since I first heard it: "When we get better, it becomes a gift to others."

If you want to be a better parent, spouse, coworker, or leader, it starts when you choose to keep improving and working on who you are.

> **It starts when you choose to keep improving and working on who you are.**

Since I travel over a hundred some days a year, at one time, my eating habits got a little out of control. I would skip breakfast and buy junk food at the gas station to keep me going on my drives. And then I would order room service around 9 p.m. and eat a large portion of fatty foods before bed.

I put on my pants one day and realized I needed a new pair. I looked in the mirror and didn't like what I was seeing. So, in order for me to feel good about myself, be healthy for my family, and have healthy energy levels, I needed to make some improvements to my eating habits.

> As I got more energy, it became of a gift to me and to others.

I started researching how to lose weight and also how to eat better, so I would be full longer and not have crazy cravings before I went to bed. I needed to lose over fifty pounds, and eating well for one day here and there wasn't going to get the job done. I needed to alter my habits and create new ones. As I improved, I noticed my life got better. As I got more energy, it became a gift to me and to others.

Personal improvement isn't solely about our weight or food; it can be about a number of things. It can be about eliminating a bad habit or some influence that brings out your worst. It can be about your attitude. I can't tell you how many times people have come up to me after my speech and said, "Hey, can you come talk to my boss/wife/kids/husband? They need a new attitude."

The key to a better you is making the choice to work on what needs working on. But here is the deal: when you work on a better you, it also becomes professional improvement. Like my friend said, when we become better at who we are, we become awesome at what we do. We care more, do more, and give our best.

THE GIFT OF
Love

*I*t is said that when we look back on our lives, we will think one of two things: *I am glad I did* or *I wish I had.*

I found an interesting story in the newspaper that shared a moving story about love. The location of the story was somewhere in Florida, a place where people often deal with alligator problems. A young boy was out playing near a retention pond while his mom washed dishes and watched him through the kitchen window. Suddenly, an alligator propelled itself out of the water and snapped its jaws around the boy's leg. The mom ran to the boy in a state of panic and began the tug-of-war for her son. She was pulling him so hard, her fingernails dug into

> When we look back on our lives, we will think one of two things: *I am glad I did or I wish I had.*

the boy's arms. As others came to their aid, the alligator let go of the boy's leg. They quickly rushed the boy to the hospital, and the doctors were able to save his leg.

Years later, the local press did a story on that boy, at that point, a young man. They asked him questions about his escape from the alligator and took pictures of the bite scar on his leg, but he wanted to tell the press about some other scars he got that day. He rolled up his sleeves and showed them the scars on his arms from his mother's fingernails. He told them that he was thankful for those scars. "Every day when I look at these scars, I am grateful because these are scars of

> "Every day when I look at these scars, I am grateful because these are scars of love."

love—the love my mom had for me the day she would not let go of me and fought for my life against the alligator."

Is there someone you have wanted to spend time with but things have just gotten away from you? I recall hearing a story about a little boy named Jonny. His mother had cancer and a very short time left to live. One day, the town minister came to pay a visit and check up on the mother. They spent some time talking, and the mother made a special request of the minister: "Would you be willing to explain to Jonny what is happening to me and what will happen so he understands?"

The minister agreed and found Jonny playing outside in the yard. He asked the boy to sit next to him on the back steps. He knew Jonny was young and may not

understand all of what he was going to explain, but he did his best. He explained to Jonny how his mom was sick and that he should spend as much time with her as possible while she was still there. Jonny asked the minister how much time he had with his mommy. The minister thought for a moment, pointed over to the big tree in their backyard, and said, "When the leaves begin to fall from that big tree, that is when your mommy will be leaving you. So while she is still here, you need to spend as much time with her as you can."

Jonny nodded to convey he understood the minister's message. Weeks went by, and fall was nearing. The air became cooler, the color of the leaves began to change, and the days became shorter. The minister wanted to check in on Jonny's sick mother, so one afternoon, he made his way to their house for a little visit.

The gifts we give through our *attitude* SPELL OUT LOVE.

He pulled up a chair and sat next to the mother, who was resting on the couch and appeared weaker than she had during his previous visit. He held her hand.

"So, have you been able to spend some quality time with Jonny?"

She shook her head. "Not as much as I would like. He's always in the backyard."

"Really? Let me go out back and see how he's doing."

The minister walked out the back door, but Jonny was not in sight. "Jonny? Jonny? Where are you?"

The little boy startled the minister by shouting down from up in the big tree. "Hey. I'm up here!"

> **Love can be demonstrated in so many ways—words, gifts, time, actions, and touch.**

Looking up, the minister saw Jonny in the big tree with a huge brown bag filled with leaves and a big roll of tape.

"Jonny, what are you doing?"

Sadly, the young boy explained his efforts in one sentence. "I am taping leaves back on the tree, because I don't want my mommy to go away."

The reason I share this story is to give a moving example that we have to make the most of the precious and limited time we have with others. We have to make it count. The gifts we give through our attitude spell out love. It is not so much about how you love or when but how much others feel your love. Sometimes we get so busy, we neglect what matters most. Have you ever done that? A story like Jonny's is a wake-up call

to seize the day and use the gifts you have to make someone feel loved.

Sometimes, love shows up in the most unique ways.

One thing I do with my wife is ask her, "What can I do to make you feel more loved today?" For her, it is just a few brief minutes of my attention and some hugs. It doesn't seem like much to me, but to her, it is everything that love is.

Love can be demonstrated in so many ways—words, gifts, time, actions, and touch. It can be sitting with someone and just listening. Your presence can be an act of love. You don't need to have solutions for them; just being there is what makes them feel loved. Love can be admitting you were wrong about something and owning the situation. Love may be watching what someone else wants to watch on TV because you know it is their favorite show, even though you can't stand it. The demonstration of love is a wonderful gift. Don't hold it in; rather, step out of your comfort zone, make the time, and do something that demonstrates one of the greatest gifts we can give to each other—LOVE!

Let no one ever come to you without leaving better and happier.

—MOTHER TERESA

THE GIFT OF
Hope

We've got one rule: love one another!

–JACKIE MOON, *SEMI-PRO*

Sometimes, having a little hope that whatever is going on in life will work out for the best and that everything will be okay is the most comforting gift in the world. A little hope is like a night-light that shines in the dark. Hope gives us something to look forward to. Hope gives us strength to hold on through the storms of life. Hope chases away our fears and anxieties. A little hope can go a long way. Hope gives us a clear view of all we have to be thankful for. There have been moments in my own life when having a little hope was like getting some fresh air. I felt like I could breathe and that heavy weights had been lifted off my chest. Hope is such a powerful gift.

> **"I would like a Bible in my right hand, and in my left hand, I would like a fork."**

The following story is one of my all-time favorites. It gives me hope and helps me keep looking forward in positive ways.

Emma was in her eighties and was given news from her doctor that she was terminally ill and didn't have much time left. She invited her pastor over to go over her funeral arrangements for when the time came. As they sat at the kitchen table, Emma laid out her requests. "Pastor, when I am lying in the casket, and people come to pay their respects, I would like the Bible in my right hand, and in my left hand, I would like a fork."

Puzzled by the fork request, the pastor inquired as to why.

She explained:

Since I was a little girl, I have been to potluck dinners, fund-raisers, and elegant dinners. After the main course, when the waitstaff would remove the dishes, they'd always tell you to hang on to your fork. I always smiled, because I knew it meant the best was yet to come—dessert. And so as I lay there, I want people to see that fork and know that no matter what's going on in their lives, the best is yet to come.

Sometimes just a little hope fills our heart in such a way that, no matter what is going on, we know everything will work out in a good way. Hope is one of the best gifts we can give others.

Another story that stays with me comes from when I was waiting

> **Hope is one of the best gifts we can give others.**

to board a flight in Indianapolis. There was a young man sitting across from me who was waiting for the same flight. He looked broken and scared. He leaned over to the older gentleman sitting next to him and almost started to cry. "Excuse me, sir. I hate to bother you. I am so tired. I am a recovering addict and trying to get home. I need to close my eyes for a few minutes, and I don't want to fall asleep and miss this flight. Will you wake me up when we board?"

The gentleman agreed. It was as if that gentleman had been assigned to be the young man's guardian angel. He continued to sip his coffee and read the paper but was alert to this young man and his well-being. When the boarding started, he calmly woke the young man. I could not hear what the words being exchanged were, but the young man nodded as the older gentleman spoke to him. You could tell that whatever he was sharing was helping this young man. Perhaps the young man had hit rock bottom, maybe people had given up on him, and maybe he was close to giving up on himself. But the words of the older gentleman filled this young man with some life. It was like night and day. The boy no longer looked so scared or jittery. It was as if the words were calming him and helping him to see that despite everything going on, there was hope. From my point of view, it was a selfless act of love that filled someone's attitude tank with exactly what it was deficient of—hope.

AND NOW, IT'S UP *to You*

> Those who bring sunshine into the lives of others cannot keep it from themselves.
>
> —JAMES M. BARRIE

*I*n closing, I will say it one last time: your attitude is either in the way, or making a way, and you determine which every day.

I have highlighted the most inspiring ways to create exceptional experiences for others. It's up to you how you use your attitude every day. You can use it to hurt or heal, encourage

or discourage, give or take. It is up to you. The key point to remember is that making a difference doesn't have to be complicated; using your attitude to make someone feel special is simple and can be enjoyable. You just have to be aware of your attitude and look for opportunities to use it to make situations better. We can give the gift of attitude to anyone, and the impact it has may vary, but ultimately it is wrapped in love and meaningful to others.

> We can give the gift of attitude to anyone, and the impact it has may vary, but ultimately it is wrapped in love and meaningful to others.

Choose the way of the Attitude Warrior. If someone's attitude isn't working right, instead of getting upset and defensive, choose to give them a little bit of your attitude. Put your attitude at the top of your priority list for work and in life, and you will begin to see what a wonderful gift it really is. I hope you enjoyed this book, and if you know anyone who might benefit from it, please share your copy with them or get them one as a gift.

There are probably other ideas on how to spread the gift of attitude, or maybe you have a personal story and want to share. I love reading them. Sometimes they end up in a future book or a speech because they are so awesome (names excluded of course). Feel free to email if you would like to share: Sam@SamGlenn.com.

ABOUT THE
Author

With Sam Glenn, ***It's all about attitude!*** Sam went from working nights as a janitor—negative, depressed, uptight, and sleeping on the floor—to discovering his calling, happiness, humor, and a king-size Serta

mattress. They say the two most memorable moments of any event are the opening and the closing. Sam Glenn is widely known as one of the most entertaining and energizing speakers to kick off conferences and wrap them up. At one time, Sam's most terrifying fear was public speaking; years later, he has won multiple awards for his speeches, been named Speaker of the Year by several

organizations, and spoken to audiences as large as seventy-five thousand people at stadium events. Today, Sam delivers close to one hundred uplifting speeches a year to organizations and conference events that focus on recharging people's attitude batteries.

Sam and his family currently reside in Indiana but are originally from Minnesota. In his free time, he likes to fish, collect funny stories, and practice anger management skills on the golf course. Sam is always grateful for word of mouth, so if you enjoyed this book and know someone who might benefit from it, please spread some attitude by telling others.

To inquire about speaking engagements, email Sam's office: contact@samglenn.com.

Visit the official website for Sam Glenn: www.SamGlenn.com.

Photo Credits
Cover: Krista Joy Johnson and Vectorstate
Internals: Krista Joy Johnson and Vectorstate

Published by Simple Truths, an imprint of Sourcebooks, Inc.
P.O. Box 4410, Naperville, Illinois 60567-4410
(630) 961-3900
Fax: (630) 961-2168
www.sourcebooks.com

Printed and bound in China.
QL 10 9 8 7 6 5 4 3 2 1

CHANGE STARTS WITH **SOMETHING SIMPLE.**

Pick from hundreds of titles at:
SimpleTruths.com

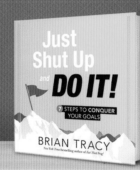

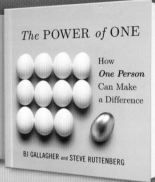

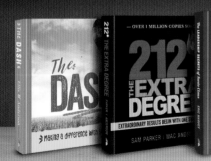

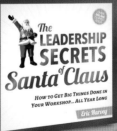

▷ Shop for books on themes like: teamwork, success, leadership, customer service, motivation, and more.

VISIT
simpletruthsmovies.com
to access our FREE library of inspirational videos!

Call us toll-free at **1-800-900-3427**